I ♥ DAD!

An Odd Squad book for the world's best DAD!

ℛℛ
RAVETTE PUBLISHING

**THE ODD SQUAD and all related characters © 2006
Created by Allan Plenderleith
www.allanplenderleith.com**

All rights reserved

First Published by
Ravette Publishing Limited 2006
Reprinted 2008, 2009.

ISBN: 978-1-84161-252-2

Sadly, Dad was unable to mow
the lawn that day.

When Mum was away, Dad wasn't too sad
thanks to his very own set of beer boobs.

Mum discovered the perfect way to get
Dad to go round the shops with her.

Dad had no idea how it had happened - one night someone or something had turned his whole wardrobe...BEIGE!

Billy made a mental note not to ask Dad
to help with his homework again.

During his round of golf, everyone was impressed with Dad's bogie.

Dad liked to do his best to make his daughter's new boyfriends feel comfortable.

When Dad wanted to treat Mum he bought
her a big bottle of bubbly.

The kids bought Dad the perfect jumper for his birthday.

Dad makes a cat flap.

Like all men, Dad handled having a cold really well.

Dad discovers something to stop his computer catching a virus.

Dad finally gets his perfect garden.

To save on fuel bills, Dad simply buys
a can of Deep Heat.

Dad discovers the new sofa was NOT fire retardant.

Dad had the perfect bedtime story to keep the kids quiet.

Dad was delighted that he'd taught their child his first word.

Although the survivors had no food and were miles from anywhere, they needn't worry - because Dad had remembered the flares.

Dad would do anything to avoid
doing the dishes.

Unfortunately during his golf game, Dad's ball landed in a bit of rough.

Embarrassed by his balding, Dad gets some hair plugs.

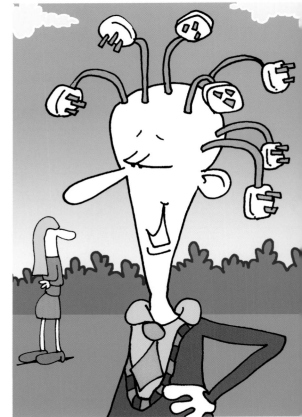

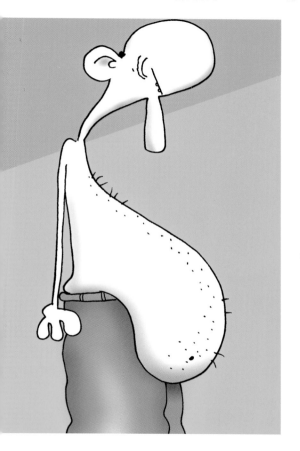

The morning after a heavy session, Dad woke up with a terrible hangover.

Dad had been under strict instructions to hold his farts in while the in-laws were visiting.

Dug walked in to find his Dad trying to play his old records on the iPod.

Dad soon learned not to tell Mum to iron quietly while he was relaxing.

As drunken Dad aimed the key for the 2549th time, he slowly began to weep.

Mum tried to persuade Dad that he was spending too much time on his mobile.

Dad discovered Mum had replaced the old dishwasher with a new model.

Dad tried to reassure his son once again - there was definitely no monster under the bed.

When Dads get older they begin to suffer from a common condition - 'ear envy'.

Once again, Dad was delighted to see the monthly phone bill arrive.

Dad finally found a place for his remote control where NO-ONE would touch it.

Fortunately, Dad had no need for expensive in-car satellite navigation.

Unfortunately, during his sensual massage, Dad relaxed a little *too* much.

Having followed the secret tunnel from a hole in Dad's shed, Mum wasn't altogether suprised where it came up.

Dad commented on how it seemed like only yesterday their little son couldn't talk or walk for himself.

Dad receives another perfect birthday gift
from the kids.

The day after Father's Day.

1. SAVE ON EXPENSIVE FUEL BILLS BY HEATING YOUR WHOLE HOME!

2. INFLATE CHILDREN'S BOUNCY CASTLES!

3. HOT ONES ARE GREAT FOR STRIPPING PAINT!

4.
GREAT FOR CLEARING SPACE ON CONGESTED PUBLIC TRANSPORT!

DELIGHT CHILDREN BY PERFORMING AMAZING PET LEVITATION TRICKS!

Dad learns the perils of plucking nose hairs.

During his long drive, Dad stopped on the hard shoulder for a quick wee.

Although it was funny at first, Mum soon became tired of Dad's levitating duvet trick.

As a treat, Mum takes Dad to his favourite extra-hot curry house.

TOP TIPS FOR A
DIY DAD

1.
BEFORE YOU BEGIN MAKE SURE YOU HAVE EVERYTHING YOU NEED.

Hammer, chisel, twelve cans of lager .... check!

Mum, what's a "CLUCKING BELL"?

Er, nothing!

F****@©*!!!

2.
ENTERTAIN THE FAMILY BY HITTING YOUR THUMB OCCASIONALLY AND SWEARING.

3.
ACT BUTCH BY COVERING YOUR FACE N DIRT, MAKING MANLY GRUNTS AND LETTING OFF RASPERS!

4.
MASK ANY DODGY BITS OF D.I.Y. WITH A SELECTION OF PLANTS AND ORNAMENTS!

Mum catches Dad looking at another woman's breasts.

Billy learns not to leave Jimmy the tortoise lying around during one of Dad's D.I.Y. projects.

USES FOR MY OLD MAN!

**1.
BIG FAT BUMS
MAKE EXCELLENT
TRAMPOLINES
FOR KIDDIES!**

**2.
STICK SEQUINS
ON BALD HEADS
TO MAKE A
CHEAP DISCO
BALL!**

3.
SAGGY BITS ARE GREAT FOR STORING TINS AND BRIC-A-BRAC!

4.
EXCESS BUM HAIR CAN BE PULLED TAUT TO MAKE VIOLIN STRINGS!

Dad was most annoyed when he returned to his car, to find a big bird dropping on it.

Dad's plan to sneak secretly into work late was ALMOST perfect.

Suddenly, Dad learns the importance of putting a nappy on tightly.

Thanks to Dad's keen observation,
the boat swerved out of harm's way.

Dad always made sure he ate his five portions of veg each day.

Other ODD SQUAD books available ...

		ISBN	Price
Book for Blokes	(new)	978-1-84161-319-2	£5.9
Guide to Love	(new)	978-1-84161-324-6	£5.9
Guide to Poo	(new)	978-1-84161-325-3	£5.9
Hot Cross Puns	(new)	978-1-84161-323-9	£5.9
I Can Make You Stupid!		978-1-84161-308-6	£4.9
The Best of Jeff and Maude		978-1-84161-294-2	£9.9
The Odd Squad's Disgusting Book for Boys	(hardback)	978-1-84161-273-7	£7.9
The Odd Squad's Big Poo Handbook	(hardback)	978-1-84161-168-6	£7.90
The Odd Squad's Sexy Sex Manual	(hardback)	978-1-84161-220-1	£7.9
The Odd Squad Butt Naked		978-1-84161-321-5	£4.9
The Odd Squad Gross Out!		978-1-84161-219-5	£3.9
The Odd Squad's Saggy Bits		978-1-84161-218-8	£3.9
The REAL Kama Sutra		978-1-84161-318-5	£4.9
The Odd Squad Volume One		978-1-85304-936-1	£3.9
I Love Beer!	(hardback)	978-1-84161-238-6	£5.9
I Love Mum!	(hardback)	978-1-84161-249-2	£5.9
I Love Poo!	(hardback)	978-1-84161-240-9	£5.9
I Love Sex!	(hardback)	978-1-84161-241-6	£4.9
I Love Wine!	(hardback)	978-1-84161-239-3	£4.9
I Love Xmas!		978-1-84161-262-1	£4.9
The Odd Squad's Little Book of Booze		978-1-84161-138-9	£2.9
The Odd Squad's Little Book of Men		978-1-84161-093-1	£2.9
The Odd Squad's Little Book of Oldies		978-1-84161-139-6	£2.9
The Odd Squad's Little Book of Poo		978-1-84161-096-2	£2.9
The Odd Squad's Little Book of Pumping		978-1-84161-140-2	£2.5
The Odd Squad's Little Book of Sex		978-1-84161-095-5	£2.9
The Odd Squad's Little Book of Women		978-1-84161-094-8	£2.5
The Odd Squad's Little Book of X-Rated Cartoons		978-1-84161-141-9	£2.9

HOW TO ORDER: Please send a cheque/postal order in £ sterling, made payable to 'Ravette Publishing' for the cover price of the books and allow the following for post & packing ...

UK & BFPO	70p for the first book & 40p per book thereafter
Europe & Eire	£1.30 for the first book & 70p per book thereafter
Rest of the world	£2.20 for the first book & £1.10 per book thereafter

RAVETTE PUBLISHING, P.O. Box 876, Horsham, West Sussex RH12 9GH

Prices and availability are subject to change without prior notice.